ENFOLDED IN SILENCE

ENFOLDED IN SILENCE:

A STORY IN ART OF HEALING FROM SEXUAL TRAUMA IN CHILDHOOD

BARBARA HUGHES

Border Press
Sewanee, TN
2013

Border Press
PO Box 3124
Sewanee, Tennessee 37375
www.borderpressbooks.com

Publisher's Cautionary Note: This book contains graphic images of sexual abuse and is not appropriate for children. Some abuse survivors in delicate parts of their healing process might find the pictures and poems triggering; readers may want to seek professional help if they should become triggered; neither the author nor the publisher are responsible for any reactions readers may have should they choose to read this book.

Ordering Information:
Quantity sales. Special discounts are available on quantity purchases by corporations, associations, and others. For details, contact the address above.

Cover and interior paintings by author, Barbara Hughes
Cover design by Martin W. Romero

Enfolded in Silence: A Story in Art of Healing from Sexual Trauma in Childhood/
Barbara Hughes.–1st ed.
ISBN 978-0984891580
Library of Congress Control Number: 2013947306

To Bob

who knows the meaning of love

TABLE OF CONTENTS

LIST OF IMAGES

FOREWORD

Enfolded in Silence is what we literary critics and teachers of women's literature and women's studies call "survivor discourse." It resonates as confessional, memoir, testimonial, and spiritual autobiography, ultimately charting Barbara Hughes' difficult path toward wholeness and acceptance after being sexually abused as a child from the ages of three to nine. Its narratives and poetry are complemented by Hughes' own artistic renderings of the experiences she relates, beginning with the stunning visual image of her troiţa (large painted Cross modeled on those she saw in Romania). Such emblems can commemorate, remind, and protest, Hughes tells us, and she begins her book with her own emblem of and protest against her childhood abuse and that of others. "I made it to be the story of my healing," she tells us, "and of what I came to believe was the grace of the Holy in the midst." From the beginning of her book, then, she blends both secular and spiritual in a compelling and graphic narrative that emerges not just as one woman's personal odyssey, but as a microcosm of all such stories, and an empowering call for others to break the silence and speak their pain. *Enfolded in Silence* is a search for that "lost time" the author speaks of in her first poem, and proof that it can indeed be recaptured in prose, verse, and art.

Abuse of course is not gender-specific, as recent chilling stories from abused boys and young men from the locker room to the church sanctuary testify. But from my perspective as a teacher of women's literature and women's studies, what is most powerful in Barbara Hughes' story is the window into the female psyche from early childhood into adult womanhood, a psyche besieged by feelings of powerlessness, worthlessness, and guilt over her own emerging sexual desires. Our culture and religions have always policed women's sexuality and tried to control it. Take this already existing situation, and add to it, the guilt of a young girl abused and ashamed of beginning to feel her own desires, and you have an explosive and potentially devastating emotional and psychological situation. One of the early poems in the book articulates this painful awareness, now filtered through the adult woman survivor, but as a child, only vaguely felt: "I sense him smiling again/believing I'd let him invade my body/believing he'd made me want it." Hughes continues to trace this shame and hyper-awareness of the violated child, even with her beloved father. Thus the narrative, in verse and prose, reveals the insidious poisoning of natural love and desires by the act of sexual abuse—a poisoning it takes decades to escape and verbalize. What a long journey it is to embrace what Hughes calls "healthy sexual love."

In my own classrooms of young women as we discuss and write about issues concerning women's lives—sexual identity, sexuality, desire, marriage, motherhood, the single life, domestic violence or abuse—I am constantly aware of what a privileged space that classroom is, and what an obligation I have as a teacher when I read my students' narratives of dawning sexual identity, or abuse at the hands of a boyfriend, lover, or parent. Women's studies classrooms invite such intimacies, and I am always daunted by students' need to confess, need to tell. These essays are of course for my eyes only. But Barbara Hughes has revealed her story to the world, not flinching from the raw details of her abuse, at one point with a wooden stake from a fence: "at the moment of greatest pain/he brought me to orgasm/cementing the permanent, unholy bond/of pain and passion inside my brain." Believing she deserves whatever pain she feels because of her own shameful and unwilling desires, the young girl shuts herself off from the world, and like the mystics who found God only after feeling abandoned by him, she begins to articulate a feminized Deity—Sophia, "God's mothering presence." This Sophia takes the form of a mother, and of various female counselors who helped Hughes through difficult periods in her life as she works through some primal, elemental fear of God/her Father's anger. What Hughes' story makes abundantly clear is how belief in a patriarchal God somehow must make way, at least in this young woman's mind, for a broader conception of "God." Enter Sophia, the Wise Women, the Healer Mother and other embodiments of female nurturing and life. It is to the female that she turns for unconditional, nonjudgmental love and comfort.

Our twenty-first century has many secular and sensationalized narratives of abuse and abandonment—some real, some fictionalized. But what Barbara Hughes adds to the mix is her own grounded spirituality made up of traditional Christianity, feminist theology, and other religious traditions. The subtexts of her story are the age-old questions of the would-be believer: "How can this be a Plan?/How can You think this works/as an Act of Creation?" or the words echoing those of Christ on the Cross: "why have You forsaken me?" Thus she broadens the scope of what might have been just another personal confession to include in her imagined audience all those who question the rightness and wisdom of unearned suffering. The hybrid genre of her narrative, then, also includes the medieval "complaint" to God about all the abuse and torture in the world. She confesses that she has taught all the theological arguments reconciling belief in a benevolent God with the atrocities we witness every day. And yet when the abstract becomes the personal, such faith wavers.

As Part I closes, the voice shifts from the personal "I" to the "we" of externalized witnesses to the pain and abuse. These "witnesses" are parts of the violated child's body that were ravaged and silenced—spine, labia, belly, heart. This poem, "Witnesses," begins to broaden the narrative beyond personal trauma and toward a more universal awareness: "now we return hobbling from the battlefield/where hundreds of thousands of little souls/die like this every day." "Witnesses" clearly maps a future journey beyond the personal to the communal, global trauma enacted every day; it serves as fitting transition into Part II of the book , "Tools for the Journey," where the author reaches out to those who have also survived or are still struggling.

"Tools for the Journey" forms a counter-narrative to Part I, as it balances the purely confessional mode of the earlier segment—the intense and necessary tunnel-vision of the child victim—with a more pragmatic and enabling plan of survival. This section is definitely a fable of our times, as it combines the language of Twelve-Step Recovery with PTSD strategies such as EMDR (Eye Movement Desensitization and Re-processing). Coupled with these physical and kinetic strategies are the more literary and spiritual ones such as journaling and praying. Part II continues the confessional mode as it reveals Hughes' other addictions and resulting conflicts—compulsive over-eating, problems with marital intimacy, "ending the illusion my parents had about my childhood." With the help of survivor groups, art therapy, counseling, making her experience public and "reclaiming my adult sexuality," as she labels one section, the author can confidently assert "I have been given my soul back, my life back." She has moved from total passivity to choice, though she emphasizes that her journey was not a smooth trajectory to wholeness, nor her story an easy one to tell. Again, the voice shifts in the last pages from the recovering "I" of the suffering child, through the "we" of the fragmented child's body parts, outward to the "you" the book finally addresses: "If you are a survivor of childhood sexual abuse or other trauma, please get help." And Hughes reinforces her practical survival strategies with spiritual direction from Psalms 84:5: "Those who walk through the desolate valley will find it a place of springs."

Read this book and know that it is not only one isolated woman's story of abuse and trauma, but a story enacted daily across the world. Barbara Hughes' story will help us remember.

Mary Ann Wilson
Professor of English and Women's Studies
University of Louisiana

PART ONE:
THE STORY

INTRODUCTION

Like so many others, I was devastated by childhood sexual abuse. My abuse involved my perpetrator sadistically causing me physical pain—sexual torture. But all sexual abuse is a form of torture, even if there is no penetration or pain. All sexual abuse is violating. All sexual abuse is devastating, especially for children. What follows is my story of what it was like and what happened to create my healing. Through painting, poetry and narrative, I try to tell what the lies were and what the truth is. My intent is that others who have suffered trauma may find validation, encouragement and hope in this story. I also write to give those who work or live with abuse survivors an inside look at the process of destruction and healing. And to offer anyone who is interested in these matters another way of understanding. The road to healing is a very difficult and arduous one. It takes time. But at the other end, there is life.

THE TROIȚA

THE TROIȚA

My husband and I took several mission trips to Romania. On these trips, I fell in love with the large painted crosses that appear in many yards throughout the countryside. Each cross has an arch over the top with painted metal angels flying around it. It is called a troiţa (troy-ee-tsa). It commemorates important events, reminds travelers of God's presence, and is a kind of silent protest against repression.

After years of working on my abuse, I decided to make my own troiţa as a commemoration of, and protest against, my childhood abuse and that of others. I made it to be the story of my healing and of what I came to believe was the grace of the Holy in the midst.

My troiţa is seven feet tall and four feet wide and is covered with a series of painted wooden icon boxes with doors. Inside each box I have painted a wood panel with a picture portraying one episode from the years of sexual violence I suffered at the hands of an older neighbor boy. Each of these panels represents the lies that I believed while I was being abused and afterward. On the other side of each of these panels, I have painted an image of the truth and of healing.

Many years of intensive psychotherapy work, prayer and art occurred between the lies and my ability to know the truth. Much of what it took for me to heal is in this book. I also had to go through my own sense of rage, betrayal, and despair about God to get to the relationship with the Holy portrayed in my troiţa.

On the outside doors of each box I have painted images of the love, grief and rage of the Holy One about my abuse. The angels also reflect God's energetic aliveness in contrast to the deadening effect of abuse. The angels protect and care for the wounded child. In the center is Sophia. Sophia is the biblical Greek for Wisdom, the feminine presence of God found in Proverbs and referred to in other places in the Bible.[1]

I found Sophia in my interior Safe Place[2] and her compassion and guidance, and that of Jesus himself, saw me through the years of emotional crisis and pain. Around Sophia are the three animals who have been my helpers and protectors in my Safe Place, and a grieving woman with the wounded child. This woman is one of a group

---

1 I have been encouraged in my understanding of Sophia by the book, *She Who Is*, by Elizabeth Johnson (New York: The Crossroad Publishing Company, 1990).

2 See page 69

of the Wise Women who appear in several other places on the doors.

They also are in my Safe Place. On the bottom door, they are grieving the terrible cost of abuse and below them are streams of their tears going into the earth.

I have had a touring show of this troiţa. It has been shown in a number of cities along with lectures and workshops for survivors and therapists. The images from the troiţa will be seen in the pages that follow, along with poems and narrative. The second part of the book is suggestions of things that helped me heal.

I am hoping that my troiţa will move people to work for the prevention of child sexual violence and to support the healing of those who have been abused. Resources for helping are at the end of the book. With this work, I am trusting that what is most personal is also most universal.[3]

---

3 This sentence I heard many times from Roses Taylor, LMFT, LPC, my group counselor.

First Door: THE WISE WOMEN

THE FALL

THE FALL

I descended into Hell
when I was three
a big neighbor boy pulled me under
the basement stairs one day
and took me there

sudden burning pain
forty-six years later
my vagina could still feel it
when the memories came

it felt like a knife inside me
but it must have been his fingers
he was jamming up into me

> Ouch, it hurts, stop,
> STOP IT OW stop it OWWWW

but I am frozen
and say nothing

on and on and on the pain

and then I sense him
smiling
smiling as he sees me in pain

I feel a wave of nausea
I want to throw up

then Rage
blind rage violence
I want to kill him

I want to do to him everything
he is doing to me
and more more more

then nothing, blank
too-quiet neverland
lost time

I come back to an overwhelming
surge of feeling
wild scary feeling
way too much for my little girl body
or soul to contain
way too much

but I am made to feel it anyway
in an act which will imprison
my passion in a torture chamber
for years and years
and years to come

I fight it at first
but then it fills me
taking me away
from the pain and terror
opening me to the core
of my neediness
waves and waves
it is everything and everywhere

> don't stop, I want it, don't stop

then only pain

Slow, sick, sinking condemnation
oozes into my belly
into my whole being
the Sentence is being etched
in my mind
"you are unforgivably bad"

I sense him smiling again

believing I’d let him invade my body
believing he'd made me want it
I am completely defeated
I want to die

Part of me came up out of Hell that day
and went on living
part of me did not

I would see that little dead girl
again and again in nightmares
staring up at me
through the waters
of a shallow stream

until four decades later
when I took the awe-full trip
back down to get her
like Jesus
descending into Hell
to pick us up in his arms
and bring us back
alive

THE LIE: YOU ARE UNFORGIVABLY BAD

I AM A CHILD OF GOD

BELIEVING THE TRUTH

It took years of intensive therapy to get out from under the belief that I was unforgivably bad—that I was bad *by nature*. I had tremendous shame about not having been able to defend myself and about the feelings that got aroused in me. It took all that time to fully believe the truth pictured here (I am a Child of God):

I am a child of God.
I am a precious being, beloved by the Holy One.
The abuse was not my fault.
I was wise and brave.
I have integrity, moral sensibility and courage within me.
I am a human being who makes mistakes and sins, and by
God's grace, works to be faithful to what is good.

Before I could believe these things, I had to come out of denial and feel the pain so long repressed. That pain was like living in a tornado. Sometimes it was terrifying. I had to cry and cry and be comforted (Comfort), over and over again. I had to find the rage that I did not know I had, and express it in every safe way I could.[1] I had to recover the spirit that had been drained out of me.

As it is for so many survivors of childhood sexual abuse, healing was a long, slow, often wrenching process. After years of therapy, I also did EMDR,[2] a process that helps program out the lies and installs the truth at a neurological level. I came finally to understand that my abuser had all the power and that I did not resist because I was frozen in terror and afraid of being hurt worse. I had also been programmed by my parents and by the culture not to make a fuss over anything. I came to know that the sexual feelings my abuser forced me to have did not amount to consent. None of it was my fault.

Before I could see myself as "a child of God," I had to work through my anger at God and my sense of betrayal. I had to deal with my fear that there was no God and no Hope.[3]

THE TRUTH: I BELIEVE THAT I AM A CHILD OF GOD

---

1 See "Safe Ways to Express Anger," p. 75.

2 See p. 86.

3 See "Healing My Spiritualty," p. 29.

COMFORT

Second Door: HEALER FATHER

THE VOW

THE VOW

I am four
I am on the sofa, cuddled up with my Dad
he is rubbing my back
when the scary waves come again
rushing into my body
just as I am feeling my love for my Dad
I let them enter my little girl heart
opening, all the way

suddenly my Dad senses something is wrong
he jumps up and gives me The Look
of disdain and judgment
I know I am bad
I am very, very bad

I cannot let my heart feel
the ripping, the break
the severing of the lobes
I make a solemn Vow
never, never to open
never to open that place in me again
never open, never, ever

my Dad carries me down
to the basement
he doesn't know it's the place of my rape
he doesn't see the terror building in my body

we are in his shop

his back is turned
he doesn't see my distress

the waves are back
this time drenched in trauma
there is a Monster within me
that I can't control
I think I deserve to be punished
I think my Dad is going to torture me
with the vice
I can hardly breathe

It seems like hours
me in agony, his back turned
until he picks me up again
and we go back upstairs
barely time to swallow the pain
I have a face to wear

THE LIE: MY SEXUALITY IS A MONSTER LIVING IN ME

THE SACRED CHILD

HEALING THE SEXUAL WOUNDS

I have worked many years to heal from the heartbreak over what I perceived was my dad's scorn of my sexual feelings. (I didn't know what "sexual feelings" were, but I thought that he believed that the powerful feelings I felt in my body when I was with him were very wrong). Because of this perception and my dad's own emotional neediness and intense focus on me, I created a wall of anger between us, hidden inside. There had been other times when my dad was holding me when I felt the feelings and they were scary and traumatic. He often egged me on to be sillier and sillier and then became angry when it was too much for him. At the very least, I was angry at him because he failed to protect me from the ongoing sexual torture by the neighbor boy.

Many times in therapy I have talked to my father in role play, written him letters I did not send, yelled, cried, raged, done painting, collage, and healing ritual. After I had done those things enough, over years, I came to understand that my dad was a good man (and he was a good father in many ways—doing a lot of fun things with us) who was acting out of his own woundedness and his ignorance of my abuse. I do not minimize my pain from the relationship, but I believe now that, in his heart, my dad wished me well.

With much hard work, I came to believe that the passionate love I felt that time with my dad was in itself good. But my fear that I would be badly hurt if I opened my heart to passion again was very deep. I can only imagine how it would have been if my father had actively sexually abused me. Millions of women carry this devastating pain.

Because of the repeated sexual violence I did experience, it has been a long battle for me to believe that my sexuality is not a monster living in me, but the sacred light of passion within (The Sacred Child). I had to do healing body work. I had to be in recovery from my addiction to abusive sexuality. I had to begin from scratch to slowly, slowly rebuild the connection between sexuality and love. It took hours and years of therapy work and the patient love of an extraordinary husband (The Vow is Broken). Being able to experience healthy sexual love while having my Inner Child feel safe was in fact one of the last frontiers of healing. It was a miracle of God's grace.

THE TRUTH: MY SEXUALITY IS A SACRED LIGHT WITHIN ME

THE VOW IS BROKEN

Third Door: HOLY SOPHIA, HOLY GOD

THE STAKE

THE STAKE

It began with dread
skin crawling
sinking, creeping sexual dread
all through my body, into my bones
spasms of fear

I was little, four or five
lying on my side on the ground outside
my abuser was sitting behind me

before us on the ground
was a piece of wood
like the top of a picket fence post,
pointed, braced to stand upright
prepared for my torture

I was to lie on top of this stake, with the point in my belly
I had to get on it myself – he was waiting for me to do this
I had to go through this ritual torture,
he made me know
because I was bad
and I had to be punished

my vagina burned with the memory of
when he tortured me before;
sexual feelings fed my shame, making
me feel in my body
the rightness of my punishment

underneath the shame, a silent little girl
was screaming

> I don't want to do it
> I can't do it
> it will hurt
> it will hurt me
> I'm so scared
> I don't want to do it
> NO NO
> I don't want to do it

I didn't know what worse thing he would do
if I did not get on the stake
he waited for me to suffer this hideous struggle

until my fear for my life
overcame my fear of the pain
and bravely I mounted the stake, its point in my navel

I don't remember the pain
not directly
(although for decades my belly burned
with the echoes of it)

I remember being clenched up against it
I remember that the sides of my body
did not touch the ground
I remember fighting, fighting
to keep the muscles in belly and arms
tight

I remember his hand on my back pushing
me into the pain
the weight of his sadistic desire, of Evil,
all over my back
pushing, pushing
controlling my pain
waiting for me to give out

to survive, I enclosed myself in a
soul-breaking shame
believing this pain, this violence to my
belly
my womb-place, my sacred female heart
center
was just right, just what should happen
just what I deserved
— at least there was some order to it
that way

I remember it going on for a long time

I remember the moment
when I knew I couldn't hold out any lon-
ger
that my muscles were going to give way
and the tender place in my navel would
take the whole weight

I remember the horror as it happened
I remember crying out in pain
then suddenly I was hovering above my
body
the pain next to me
dancing like disembodied squiggles of
light

It seemed like hours

although protected by clothes, it felt to
me
as if the stake was almost all the way
through me
somewhere in me I believed then
that I would die if I did not get away
and I could not

and at that moment
Order, Life itself
everything
was coming unglued
dizzy, nauseous
Nothingness descended
it felt as if my soul was being lost

TERROR

(One day I would remember what was
happening
while I was out of my body in terror
at the moment of greatest pain
he brought me to orgasm
cementing the permanent, unholy bond

of pain and passion inside my brain)
the next thing I remember was him leav-
ing
making me know that I had to stay on
the stake
that I would be hurt worse if I ever told
ten times worse

I remember lying impaled, alone
an aloneness so horrible
that I wanted him to come back

I remember fighting, fighting
to get back into my body
the pain filling me as I did

I remember at last,
some natural, living part of me
forcing its way up
through my shame and fear
and making me get off the stake

O God   O God

lying on my side, little, alone, crying
beginning to feel
hurt beyond hurt
hurt beyond hurt

and then slowly, fiercely
an awesome bitterness
toward everyone and everything
began to form itself in my soul
fighting, fighting
to wall off the pain, the terror, the
memory, the hurt
forever

THE LIE: MY SOUL CAN BE LOST

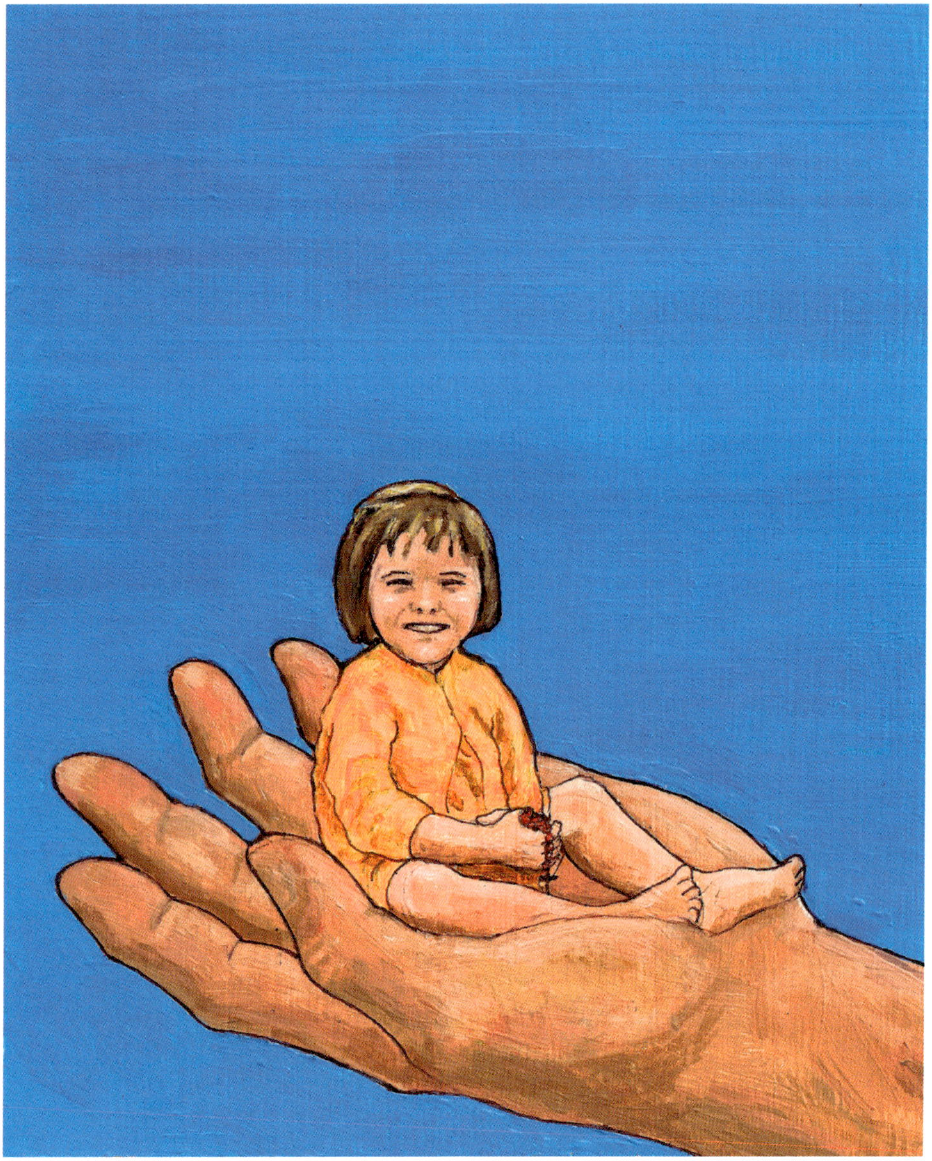

HOPE AGAINST HOPE

HEALING MY SPIRITUALITY

The image of The Stake represents the episode of ritual torture performed by the same disturbed neighborhood boy who raped and tortured me before. The amount of terror I held in my body around this trauma was immense. The red in the image represents this terror and the presence of evil that I felt. There was no blood spilt. It took many years to feel safe enough to do the healing work on this event. While I was being tortured, and in the aftermath, I believed that, not only my Dad, but God was approving of my punishment. I felt utterly abandoned, betrayed and hurt by both of them.

A wise spiritual director told me to tell God exactly what I was feeling and thinking. And so for months and months, I told it all to God (in verbal prayer and in writing), and I yelled and cried down to my bones. The Psalms that rage against God (like Ps 13:1-3) were really helpful to me, and validated my feelings. Once in prayer, I experienced God's apology to me, and another time, Jesus' admission that my abuse was a kind of betrayal by God in that God was not able to stop it.

I had to begin again with God. Sophia came to me as God's mothering presence. I began like a baby at her breast, piling pillows on my couch and drinking warm milk. Slowly, slowly I built back trust. I received deep comfort from her and I believed in her outrage and grief about my violation. Now I can see that throughout the work of remembering, feeling, and struggling, Jesus was there, guiding, strengthening and protecting me. Even with all this healing, there is a Complaint to God about all the abuse and torture in the world—a Complaint that remains.

At the point in this episode of abuse when I left my body and felt that my soul was being lost, I had an experience of the absence of God, a terrible Nothingness. For the first months of my healing, I could not let myself fall asleep because, as I would begin to slip out of consciousness, this panic of being lost would overwhelm me. I carried this terror for a long time and know that it has never completely gone away.

The previous image is my hard won Hope against Hope that we can never be separated from God's love and that even in further trauma or death, we cannot be lost. For a long time, I had to lean on the belief of my faith community. Now I have this hope against hope.

THE TRUTH: I HAVE A HOPE AGAINST HOPE THAT MY SOUL CAN NEVER BE LOST

I DO NOT UNDERSTAND

I do not understand
standing here beside a traumatized
three year old
whose personhood has just been
defeated by rape
whose soul now believes she is bad
in whose body great ruts of terror
have been permanently carved
I do not understand
how can this be a Plan?
how can You think this works
as an Act of Creation?

I know, I know
I have heard, I have *taught*
all the theological arguments
but here by this child
I can't remember any of it

all I can do is cry out in
a little girl's anguish
where were You?
how could You let this happen?
why why
why have You forsaken me?

I do not understand

no free will explanations
no bad choices explanations
not for this
not for this evil

there is nothing, nothing I can bear to-
day
only a tortured God on a cross
even begins to mean anything here
only a raped and broken God
gets to stand with us here

and don't you dare sing
triumphant praises over that
not here

weep and howl and mourn over the Rape
of Creation
that only a bleeding God can dwell
within

I can trust such a God
but I do not understand

Fourth Door: WISE WOMEN CLEARING THE SPACE

THE INFECTION

THE INFECTION

He was much older than the rest of us
and on this day, he was directing us
in a game of cowboys and Indians
I was the Indian
I was six

As I enter the memory
I am tied up, facing out
tied to a tree
he is standing next to me
commanding the game

I am terrified
hot frozen pain in every nerve ending
one of the ropes is rubbing against my
nipple
increasing my distress
my vagina and belly are enflamed
with the memories
of what he did to me before
the vulnerability is intolerable

the "cowboys" are running around me
did he talk out loud
about their torturing me
or did my body just know
what the game was about?

the children are running, yelling
I am barely hanging on, when
something changes in the energy and I
know the children are
out of control

I can feel my mind beginning to go
I can feel reality swaying, slipping
this time into a new
and terrible world

a red, hot, sickening wave
of a dread-full desire
is rising to engulf me
like the vampire with his bites
my abuser has finally infected me
with the underside of his disease
I want the children to torture me

I think the children must feel my heat
and know my desire
I feel exposed in some kind of
ultimate way

somewhere underneath
I feel profoundly crazy
and utterly ashamed

I don't know what happened then
the next thing I remember
I am alone with him
he is pressed up against me
I am still tied to the tree

he is pushing the stiffened
end of his thumb
hard into my navel
hurting me, badly
making my body relive
the torture on the stake
digging at the wound

but I am lost in it
lost in him, swallowed
I feel an awful bonding with him
as if he is the only anchor
in reality
the only thing
between me and Nothingness
soul sick
I cling to him, O God

AFTERMATH

it was a the loosening
of the ropes
that broke me open
the searing of the torture
far inside my person
the horrid swells
and vomited orgasm
swallowed now into
great dry heaves of pain

sinking slowly down
off the tree
grasping at my fetal body
I try vainly to hold together
what is left
he has deserted me here
one more rotten bereavement
I am alone

It is beyond telling
where I am
the other times
of rape and torture
of dark terror
and the rank of evil
of heartbreak, betrayal
of helpless soul-sick arousal
all are impacted inside this
little body
silent torrential rage
is twisted into sadistic, relentless self
hate
there is no going on
from here
there is no thread to cling to anymore

despair wearily wraps
its pall around me once again
I cannot stand
I cannot move

I don't have much time
before I have to wrench
myself up
in bitterness
to make it home

with each step I will shed
great chunks of reality
until I can enter Neverland
in uncomforted numbness
the seething wound
left alone to putrefy

underneath, I know
the Secret Truth
imbedded in my spirit
that Life is endless pain
and that all the rest
is Make Believe

THE LIE: I WANTED MY ABUSE

NO

OUT OF DELUSION

All during childhood, from the time I was seven or eight, I remember (and have always remembered) going off in secret to re-enact a semblence of my torture on myself. I had repressed the real abuse, and thought these episodes were from my sick imagination and my badness. Whenever the feelings of my actual torture came up, this was how I made the pain and terror go away. Many survivors of sexual abuse cut themselves for the same reason. It is a survival mechanism that keeps us in delusion (that we don't mind being hurt) and denial until we are strong enough to bear the real pain of the violation.

In my late forties, after I stopped the self-abuse (which by that time had become mostly sexual fantasies of being tortured) under my therapist's supervision, the body memories of my real sexual torture came flooding back. In therapy, I got safe enough to allow the full memory to happen in me. It was not imagining what might have occurred; it was dealing with an overwhelming force that was happening in my body, mind and spirit. I was plunged into emotional crisis, depression, panic attacks, and all that comes with finally dealing with the pain.

Despite all the turmoil, second and third opinions and the corroborating remembrances of my family, I still struggled to believe the abuse happened. My denial was iron clad. But I found that whenever I doubted my experiences, I went into dissociation and deep depression. Underneath, my heart was breaking. When I accepted that my abuse was real, even with the pain, I came into a place of wounded peace. My heart began mending. The psychiatrist I went to for a third opinion said this was how I knew it was real.

Coming out of the delusion about this episode of my abuse, I understood that I did not want to be tortured. (No one wants to be hurt). I had gone into delusion in order to keep my personality from splitting. Underneath, my soul was crying out "NO!"

THE TRUTH: I DID NOT WANT TO BE ABUSED

Fifth Door: JESUS AND ME

HE IS CAUGHT

AT MY HOUSE

My mother remembered it vividly: my walking down the stairs to meet my abuser. Someone had seen him tying me up and told. He was forced to come over with his father to apologize. My tormentor had been caught but the words stuck in my throat; my mind could not bring it up. And even if it could, I would never have said anything in his presence. He had threatened me time and time again about telling.

But I couldn't even remember—could not tell, could not ask for help, could not say anything. What I said was, "nothing happened" and my soul sank into despair. "Nothing happened" I said. I could feel the wounded part of me descending fully into oblivion. I would not find her again for decades. Now I was really hopeless. My parents never asked more about it. He was caught and they were helpless. Nothing could make it stop then. Nothing. I was alone.

Sixth Door: HEALER MOTHER

INVITATION TO EVIL

THE DOOR

I am in my front yard
I am older now, maybe eight
no one is around
he is pushing me up against a tree
there is no waiting or build-up this time
he just sticks his thumb in my navel and probes
while he stimulates me

I can't access any inner resistance or fight in me
I let myself go with the arousal and pain
in a way I never had before
now I see a tunnel coming from my belly
down into the evil
there is an open door to it
I walk through

then, when I have an orgasm, he goes away
I feel a terrible longing
I wanted him to hold me
I am devastated by his leaving
as if nothing had happened
I feel like trash
I feel sick self-loathing
underneath, I hate him, I feel rage
I feel the utter shame, the complete loss
of any remaining trace of self respect
I feel the sharp stabbing
of emotional pain
I have given in
given everything
I am less than nothing

THE LIE: I CHOSE EVIL

I AM BROKEN HEARTED

THE INNER ROOM

inside me there is a place
guarded fiercely over years
entrenched grizzly pinions
flank its entrance
and spew out venom
on any attempt at intrusion
arrows of denial and ridicule
deadly enough to cut off any tears
at the knees
in the throat
sending them back cowering
into the solar plexus

but today the gates have been breached
the protectors scrambling in reproach
inside the doors there is a room
and in that room is
barren raw and wordless Pain
pain that brooks no solace
and demands the entire allegiance of the soul
all answers and comforts and words of shame
are meaningless here
only the giving up of the body
to the great guttural sobs of the spirit

come stand beside me here
on this dark soil of desolation
abide with me and hold me fast
drench me in knowing and compassion
for I am in the awe-full sanctuary

where truth stings like fire
and I am lost in the hard labour of Grief
just do not leave me and love me through
for I am a lamb at the Heart of Pain
and you, Sophia, are the Lover of my soul

HEALER MOTHER

On the door of this box is an image of me (in the form of my Inner Child) being comforted by my therapist in her studio (Healer Mother). Lucky Man, the dog, waits at our feet. My therapist is an extraordinary woman. She was able to re-mother me within the boundaries of therapy, and she taught me how to mother myself. Her love and skill saw me through the long process of healing. My gratitude for her is boundless.

ABSOLUTION

In the episode of abuse pictured (Invitation to Evil) I saw in my mind's eye, a tunnel (pictured in red) with an open door leading into it. The door was inviting me to acquiesce in the abuse at a new level. I remember choosing to walk through the door. It was an invitation from the Dark Side.

Years later, and especially through the EMDR work, I saw that, at eight, after all the other abuse, I was beyond any inner resisting. I couldn't access the resistance. The door to embracing the evil was the only one that was open. I saw how my abuser had worn me down so far that I got seduced. I saw that ultimately it was his doing. But I was brokenhearted that I had been driven to walk through that door. There seemed to me to have been some tiny element of choice (certainly not free choice) in that moment of surrender that I needed to acknowledge, while holding on to the truth that what I did was not my fault.

Finally, my EMDR therapist asked me what it would take for me to be absolutely sure that God did not hold this surrender against me. The word "absolution" came to my mind. I went to church and received Absolution. I believe now that God has nothing but compassion for everything that I felt and did during my abuse.

THE TRUTH: I WAS BROKENHEARTED BY MY ABUSE/ GOD HOLDS NOTHING I DID AGAINST ME

Seventh Door: SOPHIA'S BLESSING

YOU A
YOU ARE DIS
RE DISGUSTING YOU
RE DISGUSTING YOU
YOU ARE DISGU
YOU AR

DISGUSTING

ENTOMBMENT

under his hand
under his watch
the belly surges come
there is no hope of stopping them
no point
no point of reference
in the growing haze
I am elsewhere
gone

I have to struggle
now in adulthood
to get to what was underneath
the cold insanity
dig for any sign of life
down there

I am lost
my holy chamber is entered
once again
now with the Killing Eye
trampled
and with these final spasms
disemboweled before him

I cannot reach anger
not even here
the Terror of this bleak
entombment
is itself stifled
a wordless death beyond tears

THE LIE: MY SEXUAL BODY IS DISGUSTING

HOLY : BEAUTIFUL : SACRED : NUMINOUS

RECLAIMING MY BODY

After all this abuse, I believed that the parts of my body that were tortured, and that had the scary feelings in them, were bad. In the abuse pictured (Disgusting) my abuser's eyes told me that my body and what he was forcing it to do were disgusting. I completely believed him.

As an adult, these parts of my body carried so much terror and shame that I couldn't have anyone touch them. At one point during my years of therapy, I went to a woman who did healing work on the body. Slowly, slowly, I was able to go through the terror in my body to a sense of peace. At my sex therapist's suggestion, I also made a tape of my own voice saying the positive truths about my sexual parts, my womb, my female heart center. I played it again and again. I read about, and looked at pictures of, the miracle of the female body. I embraced menstruation. Over many years, I came to believe that my female body was Holy, Beautiful, Sacred and Numinous. Here I am at the age of this abuse.

THE TRUTH: MY SEXUAL BODY IS HOLY, BEAUTIFUL,
SACRED, AND NUMINOUS

Eighth Door: ANGRY BEAR

DAMN STRAIGHT, I AM ANGRY

damn straight, I am angry
it's what happens
when you rape and torture people
after they scratch their way
nail by nail
out of the soul twisting
after decades of self annihilation
and despair
after the wrenching
labor of therapy
year after year after year
it's what you get
when suddenly the Spell of Dark-
ness
begins to lift
RAGE
Rage beyond
Rage

RAGE RAGE RAGE

whose fault is that?
who created such rage?
It is the Abuser
he did it
And it is the Voice of God
thundering in the
bowels
of the one w h o
w a s abused
crying out with a
loud voice
from the cross
that RAGE
that VOICE
that HOWL
exploding through to
redemption

DAMN STRAIGHT, I AM ANGRY

Ninth Door: WISE WOMEN GRIEVING

THE DEATH BED

THE DEATH BED

I am about nine
I am leading him down
the cellar stairs
each step breathing
the living proof that
I have invited him to torture me

I sink to the floor
in nauseous dread
and body heat
he straddles me, kneeling
pinning me waiting, telling
showing me my depravity
by my own hand I have done this
I have no defense
shame saturates my marrow
he is waiting
for my claustrophobic terror
to implode

I know this agony
my body has gone
here many times before

but when it begins
the pain swallows my breath
and thunders through the room
I am seeing it now
as I hover above my body

down inside
I do not want to let him
have the surrender
not this far in
not with this molten Hate
pouring into my veins

but again
he makes it come
pouring out and giving
lapping it up easily
he meets my inner eye with his glare
of perfect victory

THE LIE: HE HAS THE VICTORY

SOPHIA AND I GRIEVING

IN THE END, THERE IS GRIEF

Under the anger, under the shame, under the terror, under the denial and under the lies, there is a deep-running vein of grief in the soul. As survivors of abuse, we struggle not to feel this pain. I was afraid I would drown in it. My need for comfort felt overwhelming. Going to this place of grief could only be done slowly and carefully in therapy. But as I was able to sob and receive comfort many times over, and as I was able to move through all the barriers to my grief and stand at the bottom of my pain, I knew I was on solid ground. There, in the midst of my most profound grief, I knew that I was in the presence of the Holy. My grief did not go away, but it was sanctified, made sacred.

When I went through a year of EMDR, I saved all the Kleenexes I cried into during that time. I made little "thank you" bowls out of clay for all the people who had helped me heal. I used the Kleenexes along with sawdust and manure to smoke fire the pots. The Kleenexes burned into the pots. I had blessed my grief.

Grief for a childhood of abuse never really goes away. For those who have the opportunity to heal (and many don't or can't), when the major work of healing is done, the grief becomes an undercurrent that rises and falls amidst a life that has a landscape of happiness and times of deep joy. As long as we honor the pain when it comes up, it makes us human and accessible to others. It makes us sensitive to suffering and, along with anger, fuels our desire to make a difference about abuse and torture in the world.

NO VICTORY

Ultimately, my abuser did not win. He caused great harm, some of it irreparable. But there was no victory. He committed suicide in his thirties. After this last episode of abuse (The Death Bed), I moved away from the town where he lived. But I took my abuse with me. Many years later, I fought through, with God's grace and much help, to find my truth and my self. The price was very high (for my abuser and for me). Somewhere inside, my abuser must have been an anguished soul. Now he is dead. I have been deeply scarred, but I am alive and well. I have come, only after many years of processing (raging at him until I didn't need to rage anymore and doing a ceremony of burying him), to a place of not wanting to stand between him and God's redemption.

Forgiveness, however, is a very tricky business for survivors of childhood sexual violation.[1] Children who are being sexually manipulated (and the adults they become) find every reason to excuse the behavior of their abusers and blame themselves. Such toxic "forgiveness" keeps them trapped in victimization. In order to heal, it is vital that survivors redirect blame away from themselves, first toward their abusers and those who failed to protect them, then toward evil, and finally toward the God who created the cosmos.[2] To demand that they forgive their abusers as any prerequisite to healing or to God's mercy (or ours!) only invites a false and damaging resignation.

Being clear that they were not to blame and forgiving themselves is the first and primary task of survivors of abuse. I believe it is all that is required in this life. If any kind of forgiveness for the abuser comes, it is never something that minimizes or excuses the abuse. It doesn't mean that all anger and grief are gone. For me, it was being willing to stand aside and leave things to God's justice. It meant wanting to live, for my own sake, in a universe where ultimate forgivenness was possible.

The experiences of the Holy and of healing that I have described in this book have not led to any simple sense of victory for me either. The cost has been too great, for me and for others. And although we heal on many levels, the wound to our soul remains. And we carry in our hearts the knowledge that others are being violated and tortured all the time all over the world. I am also aware that I have had many opportunities for healing work and gifted healers. I have had the faithful support of a husband, family, friends, a faith community and good spiritual guidance. Many survivors are not so fortunate.

THE TRUTH: HE HAS NO VICTORY OVER ME

---

1 See also *The Courage to Heal* by Ellen Bass and Laura Davis (New York: Perennial Library, 1988), chapter on "Forgiveness?" pp. 149-154.

2 Some survivors are blessed during their abuse and all through their lives with a sense of God's presence and love. They do not seem to need to feel anger toward God.

I KNOW MY TRUTH

WITNESSES

we have been in the abyss
knit down into the sinews of a child
raped and tortured
over years

we slipped in the cartilage when her inner spine gave
aflame with terror at the endings of her nerves
we burned in the tender labia as her childhood was breached
and were deep in the wombheart when the bludgeons ripped the door
we have abided with her there in the forever Gape of Tears

we have traced the brutal convulsions of her mind
and known Shame in the lining of the soul
we were in the pupils as her eyes beheld Hatred
evil aimed at the core
we were in her ventricles when the heart was gored
and felt the tearing of the flesh

we were imbedded in the belly as the torrents came
swimming the mind and engorging themselves with shame

we held on with her tendons till they could hold no more
and endured the horror as the gross Hurt took us
we were right there in the eye of the pain drenched orgasm
we saw the darkness coming

we were there in the body when she left it
and we sailed with her to the evil place
we traveled in the void and became lost with her
in the Nothingness beyond terror.

we heaved in the stomach of the after-pains
we ate on bile with her
face down in the dirt
and vomited up our own remains
the swollen demolition of a little soul

our cavities groaned with her Ache for comfort
of mothering denied, and Grief lodged in the throat
we screamed in the silent hysteric of rage
the boulder in the thorax

we were there when it happened again and again

we grew our tissue into the paths of trauma with her

we were skin against rope
our backs molded to bark
the day the universe tilted and the Devil came to call
promising elixirs

we went with her into the cave of self violence
of rancid desire and hideous relivings
we swallowed the cup with her every time
and chronicled the systematic poisoning of love

we witnessed the darkness descending on a spirit
we were there when the sun went under

now we return hobbling from the battle-field
where hundreds of thousands of little souls
die like this every day

what do we do now?
what can we do
but hold each other and weep
we will beat our drums and tell our story another day

today we grieve until our bodies fold in silence
we have been witnesses

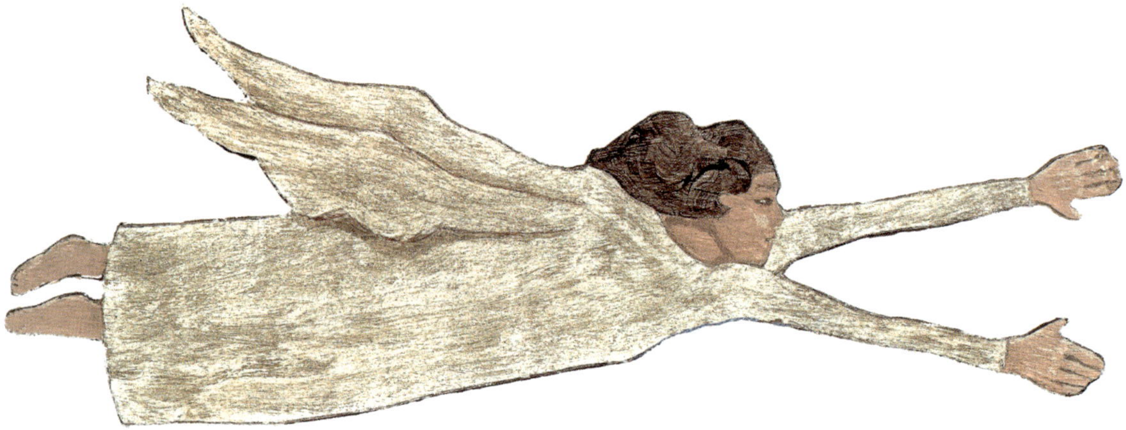

PART TWO:
TOOLS FOR THE JOURNEY

INTRODUCTION

What follows are things that helped me in my healing process. Each person is unique, and my experience is flavored by my personality, my situation, the nature of my abuse, and my religious tradition. I offer these ideas as others have offered theirs to me in the belief that it is together that we heal. Many of these ideas I have received from the therapists I have worked with over the years.

CREATING A SAFE PLACE

Creating a Safe Physical Place to Be: At first, I made a small place in my bedroom with a little rug I put near a wall, and a sacred, healing picture on the wall, low and near the floor. Above the picture, I put a cross, and on the rug I put a candle, little symbols from nature and little objects from my childhood. I would sit on the floor in front of this place and feel safe. Later, when we moved to a new house, I gave myself a loft area. It had cushions and throws to wrap up in, lots of light (both natural and artificial), warm colors and many healing images in pictures and sculptures (like a mother giving comfort to a child). I had pictures of myself as a child, Psalm 121 in calligraphy, lots of stuffed animals, children's books and healing books. I posted four sentinels (small sculptures of strong animals) at the corners of my space.

It was a place to go to cry or rage, to weep with a friend, and to do healing rituals. When I was scared and needed to feel safe, I would lie in my space, curled up with stuffed animals and quilts. I went there at night when I couldn't sleep. I had my survivors' group there for overnights. It was a space I walked by every day, and the healing images kept calling me back to my journey, especially when I was on a self-abusive track. I also put in my space some images that symbolized freedom for me, like a picture of a woman riding a horse, full out with hair flying. These images reminded me of where I was going, when I felt lost forever in the pain.

Creating a Safe Place Inside: With my therapist's help, I created an internal Safe Place in my imagination. I could close my eyes and go there whenever I needed to. For me, it was a cave underground that opened out into the light and the sea. Around me there were always my special animals: Mother Bear to protect me; The Elephant, who, like the Indian god, Genesha, kept walking through any obstacle and clearing my path; and The Lioness, who gave me power. Jesus was always there for me as friend, and a Wise Woman was there to guide and comfort me. Beyond me was a circle of Wise Women around a healing fire.

They held my pain always in their memory and contained my fear and rage. The Wise Women were always there, doing their healing work, even when I was elsewhere. Also present was Sophia who gave me her guidance. And of course, in her lap was my Inner Child. My child-self lived there, but I also left her there to be protected when my adult self had to do difficult things.

I got to my inner place by closing my eyes and counting down slowly from 10 to 1, breathing deeply with each count, as my therapist taught me. I went there when I was panicked, or when I felt disassociated and needed re-grounding. I went there when I knew I was going to have to deal with scary things, or when I needed comfort. I could get wisdom from my inner guides there, and I could find and listen to my Inner Child. It was a place of power from which I could prepare for troublesome situations, and where I could reach my Higher Self and know what I really wanted. It was a place where I was safe from self-abuse. It became a crucial part of my healing.

Taking it with me: I had a small box with tiny china animals from childhood, a little picture of a child being comforted, a candle and a cross. I took the box with me when I traveled to remind me of my journey and to be a symbol of my Safe Place. Around the box I put four little stones to remind me of my boundaries and to claim God's protection for them.

NURTURING MY INNER CHILD

When I began the healing process, I hated looking at pictures of myself as a child. I was ashamed of her and even hated her. I kept her far away from my consciousness. After my childhood abuse, my child spirit was down to a nub, barely alive. As I began to re-feel the pain of the abuse, I realized that the one having those feelings was that nub of a child within. I began to see her as a part of myself. Learning to love and care for her was a slow process, but there is nothing like that love when it comes.

I pictured my Inner Child at about four years old. Some survivors have several inner children of various ages.[1]

The Inner Child Doll: I remade the big rag doll my grandmother had made for me; I remade her to be my inner child doll. After my first memory, I committed to hold my doll and rock her every night before I went to bed. Comforting her became comforting myself as a child. I could feel her body as my body. It was a powerful way of reconnecting, of reinforcing my commitment to my Inner Child. Sometimes when I was feeling terror, I would hold her, and somedays I would lie with her and cry. The nights when I didn't want to hold her were a signal to me that I might be back in denial or self hate.

Writing to My Inner Child: I wrote letters often to my Inner Child in my journal.[2] I wrote them sometimes with my left hand to bring up the more unconscious side. I wrote to commit and recommit to her to being out of denial or minimizing about the abuse. I made amends to her when I was self-abusive or when I had shamed her. I let her know I heard how scared or sad or angry she was. I explained to her why I had to do things that were difficult for her (like medical procedures) and promised to do specific things to help her feel safe. Writing to her sometimes helped keep me from going down the cycle of betrayal, guilt, and depression.

Little Altars: I framed pictures of myself as a child and put them in places around my house and my art studio with a candle and little special objects in front of them and a cross above the frame. These became little altars of blessing and acknowledgment for my Inner Child. They caught my sight daily, and helped call me home when I was back into judging and being abusive with the child in me. Even when seeing the altars didn't help my feelings at the time, they told my Inner Child, at an unconscious level, that I honored her.

Getting Comfort: One of the most painful parts of my abuse was not getting com-

1 See also Bass and Davis, *The Courage to Heal*, 1988, chapter on "The Child Within," pp. 111-115.

2 Davis, *The Courage to Heal Workbook*, 1990, p. 268-269.

forted afterward. My child-self's need for comfort was enormous. After I had established enough trust and careful boundaries with my therapist, I would become my inner child and my therapist would hold me and comfort me and tell me what I needed to hear all those years ago. After that comfort with my therapist was in place, I did it with a few trusted friends occasionally. (Sometimes I was able to then hold and comfort them, but it was important not do that when I was in crisis and did not have anything to give). Eventually we did it for each other in my survivors' group. Only very occasionally did I ask for it from my husband. It was important that I didn't count on him to heal my Inner Child; that was my job with my therapist. These rituals of comfort healed my hurt at a profound level. It seems like a miracle that I can now say that I feel comforted for my abuse. Now it is something I offer others who also have therapy support.

A Bear: I literally could not have gone through the healing process without my faithful teddy bear, Ollie, whose fur absorbed many tears and sweats, and who comforted me through the long nights.[3]

Playtime: A while into my healing, when the women in my survivors' group had developed trust with each other, we got together and let our inner children play. We established good boundaries, and made sure the play was gentle and didn't trigger anybody. We all had an adult-self present. We read children's books to each other; we played silly card games; we blew bubbles; we climbed trees; we told stupid jokes; we spit watermelon seeds; we played dress up; and we snuggled with our stuffed animals and dolls. We laughed and laughed. It was wonderfully healing. Even without the group, doing little child things (reading a children's book or playing with dolls) was healing for me. It was giving me back what had been stained by my abuse.

A Ring of Commitment: A one point, after I had done a lot of healing work, I had a special ring made for me that symbolized my commitment of love to my Inner Child. I wear it on my right ring finger. It is a sign of a solemn vow.

---

3 You can see Ollie pictured in *Healer Father* on page 17, and in *The Vow is Broken* on page 22.

GETTING SUPPORT FROM OTHERS

Therapist: I was blessed by a skilled therapist who had good personal boundaries, and who was willing to engage with me at a heart level. I was in therapy with her for several years before I had built the trust needed to deal with my abuse. She saw me through the process with great caring and ability. She saved my life.

Later in my process, she moved away from near me and we still worked by phone and occasional visits. I also had a local therapist who continued the work with me, especially toward the end of my process, helping empower me for my being out in the world. She contributed mightily to my healing.

I have also worked with a bodywork therapist, and a sex therapist, an EMDR therapist, a physical therapist and a psychiatrist. I had a 12 Step sponsor and a spiritual director. It takes what it takes.

Group Therapy: I was in a group of four to five women and a gifted counselor for five years. We worked to create a safe place for us to deal with these very hard issues. We listened to each other's stories; we used role play; we did body work and memory work; we expressed our feelings in tears, yells, pounding, and art; we gave each other physical comfort; we learned breathing and relaxing techniques and yoga; we set goals and became accountable to each other; we tried new behaviors and celebrated successes; and we did a lot of processing of what was happening in the group. It was hard work and sometimes very painful. But we did for each other what we could not have done for ourselves. I learned to let myself be loved and to love at a new level. The connection I feel with these women now is unlike anything else.

Twelve Step Groups: I had been in 12 Step Recovery for many years for codependency and compulsive eating, before I began to work on my abuse. When I began that work, I found a 12 Step program specifically for survivors of child sexual abuse. I found their adaptation of the steps and the program very helpful. Being in the presence of other survivors at all stages of recovery was a lifeline for me. It validated my experience, gave me a road map in the dark times, gave me courage, and helped keep me out of denial. I also went for a while to a 12 Step group for sex addiction and one for ritualistic abuse.

Friends: I learned from my desperation during the panic attacks, and the long times of emotional crisis, to reach out to others. It was hard to do. I needed a lot of encouragement, but I picked up the phone. I had five friends, mostly ones I had had for years (one from college), who were either survivors or were understanding, and who agreed that I could call them when I was hurting. Only two of them lived nearby.

With each one, it was important to know (by asking and regularly checking) what their boundaries of time and emotional energy were. I was careful not to call on any one of them too often. At times I was also able to hear and support them, but not always. In one case, I wasn't careful enough and we ran into problems. But mostly, these friends were able to support me within the agreed boundaries. They validated my pain; they heard me; occasionally they held and comforted me. They were awesome, and I now find in myself a willingness to likewise support them and others. It gets passed on.

Spouse: Years of being in the crisis of dealing with abuse is incredibly stressful on a marriage. I was extremely needy a lot of the time. I was in pain a lot of the time. I was depressed. I could not respond sexually most of the time. I could tell him about my pain, but I felt too tender to hear about his pain in the situation. I often projected my low self-esteem onto him. We had many hard, entangled times.

My husband needed his own support system, and he eventually got it. He realized that spouses needed support for their own codependency issues that get triggered by the crises of the survivor, and not tips on how to be more supportive. He formed a small spouses' group with a counselor facilitator.

I learned that I was not responsible for my husband's reactions to my pain (the 12 Steps were very helpful there). I learned that no husband can satisfy the neediness of their spouse's Inner Child, and I learned to go to my therapist, groups, and friends for that healing work. I learned not to expect my husband to figure out what I wanted. I learned how to ask my husband for very specific and limited support when I needed it. We developed simple, nurturing ways to be together (like reading *The Wind in the Willows* by the fire). I learned to take breaks and do something he wanted to do when I could. We each worked our 12 Steps of inventory and amends. Even having these tools, now that the crisis years are over, I am in awe of my husband's perseverance and commitment. He is now able to tell me what it cost him. And I acknowledge myself for my hard work at staying clear with him to the extent that I could. The closeness we have now is a tremendous blessing, and much richer than anything we had before.

Family: For many survivors of abuse, the perpetrator is a family member, and the other members of the family are too locked into denial and guilt to be able to believe and support the survivor. Siblings are often in denial about their own abuse. Going elsewhere for support is crucial, as is grieving the enormous loss.

My abuser was not a family member. It was still several years after I began working on my abuse before I was ready to tell my family.[4] I had deep hurt and anger about not being protected or not being heard or helped. I had an internalized terror about telling, and an overpowering fear of abandonment. And it was hard for me to end the illusion my parents' had (I had) about my childhood. Eventually I had built up strong enough support from outside my family, and I had come to believe that the relationship with my parents could only be healed by telling them. I had done extensive therapy work on my anger and hurt toward my parents, and I was finding my own parenting for my Inner Child. Telling was one of the hardest things I've ever chosen to do.

I was very blessed by a sister and mother who believed me and were able to be supportive. They were also able to supply information that validated my memories. I had to keep asking for what I wanted from them, which broke the family rules. But it has meant that our relationships were real at last. My mother was as grateful for that as I was, despite her pain. My sister has been a wonderful support and friend. We have done healing work on our relationship. I told my dad shortly before he died (I was not aware that he would die soon), and he responded as much as he was able. It was critical for me, however, that I had solid support outside the family, and that I did not expect my family to make it right for my Inner Child.

SAFE WAYS TO EXPRESS ANGER

It took me a while in therapy to be aware of my anger. Coming to terms with my rage, the power of it, and the violence in me was scary. I did my anger work first in therapy sessions. I needed a lot of support. But I found that when I expressed my an-

4 See also Bass and Davis, *The Courage to Heal*, 1988, chapter on "Disclosures and Confrontations," pp. 133-148.

ger physically, as in the suggestions that follow, I popped out of the dark spell of the abuse and into a place of empowerment.[5]

The Anger Stick: I got a one and a half inch thick dowel—good gripping size—about two and a half feet long, and I painted it red with lots of expletives all over it. I used it to beat our futon when I was angry. Just having it around was empowering for me. Being safe, private, and not hurting myself or others were the cardinal rules. This meant being alone (or in the presence of a counselor or trusted support person) and private (out of sight or earshot of anyone), and physically safe from harm to myself, others or objects (unless they were designated for the purpose). It was crucial that there were no negative results from my anger work. One time by mistake I left my anger stick behind the door in the corner of our study that doubled as a guest room. My grown son was staying in that room on a visit, and the next morning he said to me with a grin, "Nice stick, Mom."

The Abuser Pillow: I made a bed pillow into a symbol for my perpetrator and slung it around, wrung its neck, pounded on it, and threw it away from me. When I did this work on my own, I initially needed to have my therapist know when I was doing the work, mentally be with me, and then process it with me afterward on the phone.

The Drum: I bought a drum with a wooden rim and I had each of my survivor friends draw her sign or symbol on it. I then carved the symbols into the wood. I also carved my own. I beat the drum fiercely, sometimes to rhythmic music, when I was angry. My anger had been so completely repressed for so long, that sometimes I would have to use the pounding or drumming to get to the anger ("fake it till you make it").

Recycling Phone Books: Ripping up old phone books is great!

Dancing: For me, there was nothing like dancing to some South African music to turn anger into empowering energy. I especially used songs from the Struggle to end Apartheid. These songs of freedom gave me courage, and made me feel empowerment in my body. They put my struggle in a larger context.

5 See also Bass and Davis, *The Courage to Heal*, 1988, the chapter on "Anger, the Backbone of Healing," pp. 122-132.

Giving it Voice: We lived far enough away from the next house that occasionally I went outside and bayed like a wolf and growled like a bear. Yelling from the belly - doing a primal scream—was very healing for me.

I also wrote my anger: telling it like it was, letting it all out, and scribbling hard till the paper tore. I painted my anger with red and black paint all over a big old bed sheet or paper. In therapy I had a huge (10'X10') oilcloth spread on the floor. I ripped up phone books, slathered the crumpled pages with paint and sprawled them across big paper from rolls that were on top of the cloth. I dumped paint and used my hands to spread it all over. I painted myself showing the wounds that were inside. I threw clay at the picture. I let myself do whatever was safe and agreed on. It was powerfully healing. I made collages of angry images from magazines: roaring tigers, growling bears, yelling people, and powerful colors. I made angry images in clay. Later, writing strong statements of advocacy for others to read, or showing my artwork, or speaking up publicly about abuse, became powerful expressions of my outrage.

GETTING REAL WITH THE HOLY

Dealing with My Spiritual Terror and Despair: I was a practicing Christian (Episcopalian) when I began the process of healing from abuse. But in that process, as I wrote in Part One, I uncovered my childhood terror that my soul would be lost. I relived the fear that there was no God, no hope, and no meaning. I had panic attacks and long bouts of crisis. I talked about it to my spiritual director (once in the middle of the night, which we had agreed I could do). I sometimes kept a candle burning through the night. I gripped a rosary (which I never actually prayed with). I let some words of scripture comfort me ("I will never forget you. I have inscribed you on the palms of my hands" [Isaiah 49:1]).[6] I put these words up around me. I kept going to church even though I often cried through most of the service. I clung to other people's belief. My spiritual director gave me permission to ignore anything in the Bible or in worship services that did not comfort me or serve my healing. I started to hear more comfortable words in church. I told some trusted people about what I was going through and I asked them to pray for me. It was a very hard time. Mostly, I just lived

6 p. 28.

through it, and hung on.

Expressing My Rage at God: Gradually, the crisis of Nothingness lessened and I realized that I did in fact believe in God. But what my child self felt toward God was betrayal and a sense of having been abandoned. I felt Rage. I raged at God, and felt my hurt, and let myself feel my anger.

Finding God in a New Way: Meanwhile, I was beginning to hope in unconditional Love, which was coming to me through my therapist, my group, and loved ones who did not abandon me when I had absolutely nothing to give. I was feeling a loving, peaceful, tender Presence in the moments after deep tears or rage. I was hearing about that Love in scripture and in worship, as if for the first time. And I was experiencing healing that was more than the sum of all my work. I was letting myself discover who The Holy One was for me in this journey. I was knowing God as a Mother who loved me absolutely. I felt the blessing of the Holy One on me. It is what my soul desperately needed and longed for.

I needed to get from God the nurturing and comfort I had missed. As I have said in Part One,[7] I would gather pillows and blankets and warm milk and I would snuggle up and imagine being a child at Mother God's Breast. I would try to take in Her love for me. I collected images of God that fed my soul, of God as Mother, and put them all in my space, and I made pieces in clay of God as Mother, holding me.

As a Christian, my relationship with Christ was reborn. I could see, in the Cross, a God who suffers the abuse with us and in us, and who takes on evil for us. I could see in Christ the Woundedness of God.

Healing Rituals: My soul was wounded by the abuse, and the evil that was present when I was tortured felt overwhelmingly powerful. I needed spiritual healing. I used my church's sacraments of healing many times during those years. I also created my own healing rituals. I made a big sacred circle of stones in my yard with a group of women survivors and friends. My priest (a woman) came and we did a blessing of it as

7 p. 29.

a place of healing. In one ritual, I buried symbols of abusive behavior, to give them to Mother Earth and to God for healing. In another, I put on a bear headdress that I had made as a symbol of claiming my rage and my authority. I growled and roared. I made a cross that testified to my abuse. I did the rituals alone sometimes (but with others praying for me), and sometimes with others. Writing and planning the healing rituals by myself or with others—saying it just the way it needed to be said—was healing in itself.

Daily Time with God: It helped me to take a few minutes in the morning to read a little passage from scripture, sometimes paint a mandala,[8] do some relaxing, and pray. Prayer for me was showing up, in God's presence, exactly as I was, and hanging out for a few minutes. My mind wandered terribly but I gently brought it back as many times as I needed to. I also prayed for other people then.

WRITING

The Journal: I kept a journal that I wrote in whenever I wanted to. Writing helped me get grounded when I felt crazy. I used it to express feelings, to come to terms with believing my abuse, and to listen to my inner parts. It was a way to sort out confusion, to make intentions, and to record moments of insight and wisdom. Writing meant I had a record of times when I experienced hope and healing, and I could read these passages in the times of despair. It meant I had a record of the depth of my pain, for times when I got back into denial. I made certain no one would read my journal, so it was a safe place to get real, all the way down. There were absolutely no "shoulds" about writing in it. Now I am very grateful to have this record of my journey.

Clearing: I learned a process that helped me to sort out my thinking when I got upset about something.[9] First I wrote down all the things I was saying to myself or accusing myself of (like "you are bad," "you should be over this by now") and then I went

8 See p. 81.

9 *The Clearing Process from The Life Training*, a program of the Kairos More to Life Foundation. Copyright, Roy Whitten and Brad Brown.

back and marked each statement as "true," "false," or "don't know," as objectively as I could. Then I wrote what the truth was, and what I chose to do in response. This simple process helped stop many a downward slide into a deeper depression. There were times when my depression was so great that I couldn't do the process, but I used it effectively a lot and still do.

Hearing from All My Inner Parts: I used writing to give each of my inner parts—The Child, The Doubter, The Critic, The Self-Abuser, The Warrior Woman, The Pleaser, etc.—a chance to say her piece. Sometimes I would draw a big circle, divide it into pie pieces and write what each part thought, feared and wanted about a situation. Then I tried to come up with a solution that everybody could live with (that took going back and checking it out with each one, often more than once). Then I came to a decision. Sometimes I would write a dialogue between two inner parts. In the process, I was able to see the kernel of truth in each point of view. I learned from my therapist to give new job descriptions to parts like the Doubter (his new job was to list all the objective reasons why we know the abuse *did* happen). I am convinced that survivors of childhood trauma would make great negotiators for peace treaties!

Letters I Might Not Send: I wrote letters to my abuser, my parents, people I was angry with, people I needed to confront, the president, my inner parts, etc. In these letters I would let it all hang out and speak from my gut, and not worry about the person actually reading it. In some cases, the letters were preliminary to letters I did finally send (after considerable editing). The not-to-send letter was a great way to vent and to get in touch with what the real issues were for me. When I was working up to telling my parents about my abuse, it helped me do a bunch of these trial-run letters first. When I got to what I really wanted to say, after the original telling, I read the letter to my mother.

Book of Treasures: Several years into my healing process, someone suggested that I start keeping a little book (of blank pages) where I recorded things that felt like blessings. I wrote about moments of healing, changes I saw, insights, quotes that gave me hope, things people said in a meeting, encouraging words, etc. The process of healing was long, painful and discouraging at times. This little book was a source of hope for me.

USING ART

I am a visual artist, and using art came naturally to me. But the things below are simple and require no artistic skill or experience. I have done them with survivors in workshops.

Mandalas and Painting: Mandala is the Sanskrit word for "circle," and a mandala meditation is simply a painting (or drawing, or collage, etc.) done in a circle. The circle forms a safe place—a container—for expressing things that are scary or powerful. I painted my mandalas, using my left hand (since I am right handed), so that I wouldn't worry about making a pretty picture and could let what needed to come, come. I painted mandalas for months before my first memories, and the raw vaginal wounds that kept appearing helped break through my denial. During my healing work, I used mandalas often to let my Inner Child express her feelings.

For my mandalas, I used big pieces of thick drawing paper, a big child's paintbrush, and cake tempera paint (which comes in sets at an art supply store or on line). Any paint would do. I began by lighting a candle, and I asked for healing and for protection from self-judgment. I used my left hand (non-dominant) and made a big circle (which didn't have to be perfectly round) on the paper. Then I painted as if I were about 4 years old, letting colors choose me. My paintings were usually abstract and messy, and I kept going until the colors looked like I felt. I often went outside the lines. After the mandalas were done, I was careful not to judge them, and I kept them in a safe place as precious expressions of my inner spirit.

Collage: I have mentioned that I used basic collages (magazine images glued on to poster board with rubber cement or glue sticks) to express anger. I also used collages in other ways. The trauma of abuse is so global in feeling and effect, that the collage gave me a broad panorama in which to express myself. In a collage about my grief, I could use pictures of great waterfalls and ocean scenes to portray the depth of my sadness.

Years into my healing, I felt moved to make a collage of each of my major episodes of sexual torture. I did these collages at home, one at a time, over a period of time, under my therapist's supervision. I took time for each one, slowly gathering magazine images, and I made a ritual out of the making of it. As I was compiling the images, I covered them with a healing picture or cross when I wasn't working on the collage. I asked people to pray for me. It was hard to do, but I was surprised at the peace and resolution I felt afterward. When I was ready, I showed them to my therapist, my group, trusted friends and my sister. Pictures speak louder than words, and sharing these collages was a powerful way of being heard.

Clay: I am a clay artist, so I had ready access to clay and was able to fire it. But it is often the process of working with clay, even if it is not fired, that is powerful. Sometimes local potters are glad to fire small pieces for people who don't have kilns, and they know where to buy the clay. Because clay gets all over, it's best to do in a garage or basement.

Sometimes I used a dinner knife (not sharp and being careful not to hurt myself) and stabbed a block of clay to express anger. Other times I tore off pieces of clay and threw them against the outside walls of an old shed in our backyard. Sometimes I just squeezed and mashed the clay in my hands. Letting my left hand lead, I let my Inner Child make little figures that expressed her sadness, her emptiness, and her brokenness. These crude, simple figures are now a strong testament to her pain. I also made simple figures that expressed what I needed, like being held. I put these pieces in my safe space to comfort me.

Making Sacred Objects: Earlier, I wrote of the drum I decorated with carved symbols. I also made a shield as a symbol of protection. I used clay (but it could have been wood) and covered it with painting and dried leaves that I then glued on.

I made a small cross (before I made my troiţa) out of wood and covered it with symbols and words about my abuse. I got a wooden box at a flea market and put the cross inside it. I decorated the inside and outside of the box. I put it on the wall as a kind of tabernacle. I would open its doors and light a candle at times of remembering (being sure to watch it and blow the candle out).

I glued natural objects on the trowel I used for burying things in my rituals, and I hung it in my safe space. I made a ritual of making and decorating each of these objects. They became ways of honoring and sanctifying my pain and my process.

RECOVERY FROM ADDICTION

Many, if not most, survivors of childhood sexual trauma become addicted in some way. It is a way to keep the pain at bay. And then it takes on a life of it's own.

The First Step: From childhood, one of the ways I coped with my abuse was with numbing behaviors that later became addictions. I ate, I overworked (or over-busy-ed), and I acted out some form of my abuse on myself (in childhood, physically and later mostly in sexual fantasies with some acting out). It was important to understand the positive role these behaviors had played in my survival and the ways they were attempts at comfort. But they were now keeping me in denial, besides hurting me in other ways.

I was already in 12 Step Recovery for codependency and for my food and diet addiction when I began to work on my abuse, and I was beginning to clear time from my overworking to let myself feel. But I could not get to the true feelings associated with my abuse as long as I was abusing myself or using fantasies of it sexually. The self-abuse was a kind of altered state in which I lost touch with all self-care, all morality, and all feeling. It was when I tried, with my therapist's supervision, to stop acting on it, that I began remembering and feeling. Withdrawal was hell, and I needed help to come up with the willingness not to pick it up again.[10] I had to admit that I was an addict, and could not stop on my own. I needed help from a power greater than me, and the support of the group.

Therapy and 12 Step Recovery: Because my addiction to self-abuse was so connected to my real sexual torture, I needed both 12 Step Recovery and therapy, working together, to deal with it. The 12 Steps gave me a road map for letting a Higher Power help me, and steps for getting back in charity with myself and with others. 12 step literature kept me honest about the rationalizations I had developed over the years for acting on my addiction. The steps gave me time to mourn the loss of the comfort my addiction had given me, and to become "entirely ready" to let it go. In regular meetings, I got support, tools and wisdom from people who were living in recovery one day at a time.

10 The book, *Living Sober* (New York City: Alcoholics Anonymous World Service Inc., 1976) was very helpful to me.

Therapy helped me deal with the fallout of stopping the addictive behaviors, and helped me find the underlying feelings and needs that I had to address. I learned new ways to get comfort, to feel safe, and to take breaks from the pain. I worked at healing the part of me that wanted to hurt myself. I realized, however, that no amount of therapy would "cure" my addiction: that is, enable me to abuse myself, and not become addicted. Addiction has its own dynamics. I needed both therapy *and* 12 Step Recovery.

Gradually, as I began to heal and to come out of denial, I experienced how far I was thrown back into depression, low self esteem and pain when I acted on my addiction. It hurt either way, but one way was pain that led to healing, and the other, pain that led to death. It has been, and is, a long, slow struggle, and I absolutely couldn't stay with it without my groups, and a way to call upon a Higher Power. I have been abstinent from self-abuse and fantasies of it for twenty years now, one day at a time. Recovery feels like a miracle each day.

Every Day, A Choice: Now, despite all my healing work, I can still throw it away and miss being alive, if I choose to act on my self- abuse addiction. It is always there, and as an addict, I am always vulnerable. So, the need for these tools goes on. With support, I can choose life for today.

TREATMENT FOR DEPRESSION

Understanding the Disease: After years of hard work in therapy and much healing, I was still suffering with depression. I was resistant to admitting that I was clinically depressed and needed treatment. Finally, I was able to hear that childhood trauma can wear out the ability of the brain to transmit the chemicals needed to stay emotionally healthy – that my depression was, in part at least, a neurological condition that no amount of therapy might be able to fix.

Treatment: I went on an antidepressant fairly early on, but looking back, I think I waited too long to keep at it until I found drugs that really worked. I think I could have lessened the time it took for me to heal. Eventually, I went on a lengthy period of adjustment. I had to try different combinations of drugs to find something that was effective. When I found that combination, I felt normal for the first time in my life. I could certainly still feel my pain, but coping with it was very much easier, and clearer. I could do my therapy work more effectively. The medication did not set up a false happiness. I could still feel down sometimes and still needed to use my tools to stay clear. But the tools worked. The medication helped my brain function normally, whatever I was feeling. While our understanding of depression and its treatment continues to evolve, I am very grateful today that treatment exists.

There are side effects. I have what they call "hard to treat depression" and I am on a lot of medication. The medication has a dulling effect on some of my alertness and passion. It is a trade off that I do not like, but that I choose to live with. The dulling effect of depression is far worse. Depression takes all the joy and hope out of life.

COMING HOME TO THE BODY

Reconciliation: The first step in ending the enmity I had with my body was to be clean of addictive self-abuse, one day at a time. From there, I listed all the destructive things I had done to my body—to each part of my body—and I made amends.

Learning to Listen: My body had been screaming at me for years, in colon problems, mysterious rashes and pains, accidents, vaginal pain and fatigue. I had learned lots of ways to ignore and override these cries for help. Now I had to learn to stop and breathe and listen when my body cried out. It was uphill work, but I slowly learned to be with my physical problems in a compassionate way, instead of being angry with my body for not functioning properly. Besides getting the necessary medical help, I learned to make the time to deal with the underlying distress. I let the hurting parts of my body speak to me in my journal and tell me what they needed me to hear. Not all of my medical problems had a source in trauma or emotional pain, but I learned to listen to that component when it was present.

PTSD: As I became un-numb, I had to cope with my Post Traumatic Stress Disorder. When my abuse got triggered, I felt frozen, cold, numbing in my limbs, locked jaw, vaginal pain, fast heartbeat, shaking and disturbed breathing. After much work, I began to accept this part of me with compassion also, and to not shame myself about it. I learned to be careful about not triggering myself unnecessarily. I was careful about books that I read and movies that I watched. I learned to stop reading or watching things if I began to get triggered. I learned to prepare ahead for necessary medical procedures that triggered me: I talked to my doctor and we worked out a plan with the technicians to minimize my distress, and to put me back in control in the procedure.

Tending the Wounds: After I re-membered each part of my abuse, I found a way to minister to my body in the places I had been hurt. I made a ritual of applying healing creams and bandages, where possible. I anointed myself with oil. I went to church for anointing. I once went to bed with tea and a heating pad, and pretended I was in a hospital. I got comfort from others as I have described.

Body Work: After I had done the bulk of the intense work on my abuse, I went to a therapist who helped me be present in my body at a deeper level. I discovered that parts of my body stayed frozen in fear. As she helped me let go, powerful emotions were released. At first it was very hard work feeling the emotional pain at this level, but when the feelings flowed through me, I experienced an extraordinary peace. I slowly learned better how to feel my feelings all the way down and out, so they did not get stuck in my body. It's still hard to do.

EYE MOVEMENT DESENSITIZATION AND RE-PROCESSING

EMDR is a treatment for Post Traumatic Stress Disorder.[11] It has been used effectively for veterans coming back from war and for others who have experienced trauma, including survivors of childhood sexual abuse. It is a process that stimulates opposite sides of the brain (my therapist tapped alternately on my right and left knees), and breaks up the neural pathways that go from the trigger to the reliving of the trauma. While the opposite sides of the brain are being stimulated, the therapist takes the

11 See Francine Shapiro and Margot Silk Forrest, *EMDR/ The Breakthrough Therapy for Overcoming Anxiety. Stress and Trauma* (New York City, NY; Basic Books, 1997).

client back into the feelings and thoughts of the abuse—back into the trauma—but with some protective distance between the client and it. While there, the client is able to see things differently and begin to modify the beliefs that went along with the abuse (like "it's all my fault"). The process is continued until the old pathways are cleared. After that, the positive beliefs (the truths) are installed by the same process.

It is very hard, wrenching work at times, but the results are amazing. Initially, when I had finished the EMDR process, I felt depressed (partly a factor of my medications not working). It took me a while to realize what had happened, but the power of the devastating lies and the potent feelings of the abuse were dramatically lessened. Feelings could of course resurface but not in the same kind of traumatic way they had before. The symptoms of PTSD were greatly reduced. The abuse became a memory (one that I had deep feelings about) and not a present trauma. There are therapists specially trained in EMDR. It is something that requires this professional training. I also had my regular therapist in the room to support me.

I did EMDR ten years after I started working on my abuse. In some ways, I wish I had done the EMDR sooner, but, given the depression, it took me time to be ready. It is a powerful tool, and has made a huge difference in my healing. In my heart, I no longer believe the terrible lies that came with my abuse. Sometimes they get triggered but I can much more easily process them most of the time. There is still a frequent flow of self-criticism that remains, but it is not at the same level and I have the tools to deal with it.[12]

RECLAIMING MY ADULT SEXUALITY

All of the tools I have mentioned contributed to my sexual healing. I was not ready to deal directly with my adult sexual life until I was through the crises of dealing with my abuse.

Making Space: My sexuality had been drenched in images of pain and violence. I needed to first clear the deck by being abstinent from self-abuse and fantasies of it (12 Step Recovery). I needed time out from having intercourse in order to heal and

12 See "Clearing," p. 79.

start again.

Re-imaging Sexuality: I made a collage of positive images of sexuality and put it in my safe space. I found other pictures that connected sex with love and tenderness, and I put them where I could see them often.

Therapy Help: Eventually, after doing the bodywork for some time, I felt ready to go to a sex therapist who specialized in healing from abuse. She gave me more tools for my own sexual healing, and she helped my husband and me rebuild our sexual relationship. I learned how to make myself safe in sex, and I got the courage to be honest and to stop if I was uncomfortable or got triggered. We learned new skills for talking about sex and for saying what we wanted. We learned gentle touch. We made a special time and a new place to begin making love again. I had always had pain with intercourse and I got help from a special physical therapist who helped me learn how to alleviate the pain through pelvic exercises. As we started over slowly, I was able to experience intercourse without pain and to enjoy the experience as an act of love. It took time and the progress was up and down. Sometimes I got triggered. I almost never do now. Lovemaking has become a time that nurtures and feeds me. It seems as if the impossible has happened.

WHAT MAKES IT WORTH THE PAIN OF HEALING

Healing is hard, hard work. The inner pain we touch and re-feel can be horrendous. Speaking of it being “worth it” somehow minimizes the cost of healing. But the healing that comes is precious beyond words. All I can say is that if I had not done this work, I would still be trapped in self-abuse and the cost of holding the pain inside would have become greater and greater physically, emotionally and spiritually. If I had not done the work, I would not be where I am today. And that is everything.

CONCLUSION

This has been a hard book to write. I have had to be very careful with my Inner Child. Putting all this out there has been really challenging for her especially. It would be much easier to stay silent. But a big part of me needs to speak out. I do it because it is her truth and because I hope it will help others. My Inner Child has been very brave.

Life is blessed now—rich and full. My abuse is no longer a heavy stone upon my heart. It is in my heart but it sits quietly there most of the time. Except in the writing of this book, or in lecturing or doing workshops, my abuse is seldom on my mind. There were many years when I thought that a time of just feeling okay would never come. Now each day is precious. There is a lingering sadness deep within. I hurt for others and for all the injustice and abuse in the world. But there is also laughter and joy and silliness.

I have been given my soul back, my life back. It is "the pearl of great price" that is worth everything. One day at a time, I want to live life, fully. I was told not to quit before my miracles. It was true.

I do a lot to maintain my healing. I frequently check in with my Inner Child by dialogging with her in my journal in the morning, and spend special time with her once a week (holding my inner child doll and playing with her little treasures on my altar). When she is upset, I listen with compassion and I do not shame her. In the morning, I also repeat some of the affirmations and truths I learned in EMDR, tapping opposite shoulders as I say the words. When anniversaries of episodes of my abuse come up (or just when the pain resurfaces), I stop and tend to what is going on inside. I do simple rituals and listen to my Inner Child. I let myself feel my feelings all the way down. I pray and make Eucharist.

I am very, very blessed with a wonderful husband and family who bring me great joy.

I now lead retreats for women survivors of childhood sexual trauma using art.[13] I do personal art reflection with survivors, and support individuals who are going through healing. People who have been abused seem to find their way to me. It is like that for most people who have been through the healing process. The work is fulfilling and redemptive.

13 See barbarahughesplace.com.

I teach art and spirituality workshops and classes. In the years of this teaching, there has never been a workshop or class in which at least one of the participants wasn't a survivor of childhood sexual abuse. One time, every one in the class had a history of trauma.

My husband and I have taken a number of mission trips in addition to our times in Romania. I have gone to Haiti and most recently we both spent two separate semesters teaching in Tanzania in Eastern Africa. On some of these trips we have taught about addiction and codependency. My heart is full. And much of my time is doing my own art in my studio.

Despite the "complaint" that endures, I am reconciled with God. I feel loved and loving. My Christianity (well grounded in great feminist theologians like Elizabeth Johnson and Elizabeth Schussler Fiorenza[14]) is a big part of my life. And I now embrace the masculine part of God as well as the feminine. I fall far short of living into my faith. But God is generous.

The sexual violation of children is a huge and devastating reality in our world. Organizations dealing with child sexual abuse estimate that at least one in four girls and one in six boys (some estimates say one in three girls) will be sexually abused in childhood. It is an ongoing global atrocity. A woman who supervised a domestic violence shelter told me that she estimated that ninety-five percent of the women there had been sexually abused as children. In addition to the toll on individual lives, the cost to society is enormous. As a people, we must keep breaking the bonds of denial and work actively to prevent and treat the problem. Some resources are at the end of this book.

If you are a survivor of childhood sexual abuse or other trauma, please get help. Find a therapist you can trust over time. Be patient and get all the support you can find. This healing work will be the hardest thing you have ever done since childhood—and the most rewarding. There will be dark days. But you will also find grace upon grace. ("Those who walk through the desolate valley will find it a place of springs" Psalm 84:5). Knock on every door and get the professional help you need. Get a treatment for your depression that works, and consider an intervention like EMDR. It may take you less time to heal that it did for me (but it takes the time it takes). The love you will find inside will be more than your wildest dreams. Each of us is of great value

14 Elizabeth Johnson, *She Who Is*, 1990, and Elizabeth Schussler Fiorenza *In Memory of Her* (New York: The Crossroad Publishing Company, 1983).

and deserves healing. Your healing will be a light to the world.

ACKNOWLEDGMENTS

Much of what I have learned about healing comes from my work with my primary therapist, Elizabeth Rucker ATR. Some of the things I have written about were her suggestions. I learned about doing mandalas initially from her. I learned about making my Inner Child feel safe. I learned about expressing anger. She helped me deal with my inner parts. She is an art therapist, and encouraged me in my art, as well as in many other ways. As I have said, she was willing to re-mother me, and I learned to mother myself from her. Not only do I acknowledge her contribution to this book; I owe her my life.

I had other therapists who were also instrumental in my healing and in contributing to the contents of this book. Betty Philips LMHC was the local therapist who helped me in the latter stages of my healing. She was compassionate toward my pain while always holding up the hope of empowerment. Judy McClung MA LMFT was my EMDR therapist whose gentle wisdom and love got me through the process. Along with Elizabeth, she taught me how to act with compassion toward my Inner Child. Her work with me made an enormous difference in my finding peace.

Roses Taylor LMFT, LPC was my group counselor providing space for much of my healing and some of her ideas are in this book. Besides Elizabeth, she taught me how to find safe ways to express anger. And much, much more. I have also to thank the precious members of that therapy group. My sex therapist, Ginger Manley MSN APRH, gave us invaluable help in finding our way to real sexual love, and her wisdom is recorded here. My spiritual director, Mary Avram, helped show me the way back to God, and I have shared her prayerful suggestions. She was an important part of my healing.

I have especially to thank my supportive and generous husband, Bob Hughes M Div PhD[1] for his love, understanding and encouragement as I worked on this book, and on my healing in general. And for stepping aside and letting me do it. I have also to thank my dear sister and author, Susan Puett,[2] who gave me support along the way as she does so wonderfully in the rest of my life. I have a recovery group who remain

---

1 Bob Hughes is the author of the award winning book, *Beloved Dust: Tides of the Spirit in the Christian Life* (New York: Continuum, 2008). In this book he brings the themes of liberation and healing into his study of the spiritual life.

2 Susan Puett is the author of *In Pursuit of Liberty* (Baltimore: Publish America, 2004). She is now working on a book on science and art in Renaissance Florence.

anonymous and its members have helped me more than they know in the process. Other friends have given me courage: Hannah Anderson, Cindy Potter, Tricia deBeer, Janet McDonald, Betsy Strong, Sr Elizabeth Mills, Betsy Poist, John deBeer and others.

I want also to thank my parents who loved me dearly and only wanted the best for me.

My editor, Kathy Hamman, deserves many thanks for working through illness. Martin Romero worked hard to match the colors of scanned images to the original paintings, and I appreciate his patience. I want to thank my publisher, Border Press, and Vickie Sullivan for all the cheerful hard work done on behalf of this book. I want to thank Diane Moore for her input as well as Isabel Anders. I want to thank Henry Hamman for his initial help, advice and hard work getting me going on this book and for his suggestions concerning page design.

RESOURCES

Know the facts: Organizations dealing with child sexual abuse estimate that at least one in four girls and one in six boys (some estimates say one in three girls) will be sexually abused in childhood (http://www.parentsformeganslaw.org/public/statistics_childSexualAbuse.html and casacares.org). Ninety-three percent of abusers are someone the child knows. Forty-seven percent are family members or extended family members. Thirty-nine million people are the victims of sexual abuse in the US. Twenty percent of them are under the age of eight. (stopcsa.org).

Resources for the Prevention of Childhood Sexual Abuse

There are organizations that do good work in prevention and treatment for childhood sexual abuse. All have ways to contribute and many have ways to volunteer.

https://www.childwelfare.gov/organizations gives a list of organizations dealing with childhood sexual abuse.

Darkness2light.org gives a list of five steps to preventing child sexual abuse, and has developed a Steward of Children training program to help adults protect children from sexual violation (adultsprotectingchildren.com).

Rape, Abuse and Incest National Network (rainn.org) is the largest organization working against sexual violence.

Stop It Now (stopcsa.org) is committed to stop childhood sexual abuse and to treat survivors.

Center for Prevention of Abuse and Violence (casacares.org) has prevention programs for schools as does safersociety.org.

You are required by law to report childhood sexual abuse. Early intervention can make a huge difference for children. And of course, getting a perpetrator of the streets can save many children.

To report abuse call 1-800-4-A-Child (1-800-422-4453) and they will provide the number for the state where the abuse took place.

Resources for Adult Survivors of Childhood Sexual Abuse

OpenDirectory (http://www.dmoz.org/Society/Support_Groups/Sexual_Abuse/Survivors) has a list of sites for adult survivors.

For retreats for women survivors of childhood sexual abuse and other trauma, see my website at barbarahughesplace.com.

malesurvivor.org has resources for men who were sexually abused in childhood.

Therapists

Elizabeth Rucker ATR is no longer taking new clients.

Judy McClung MA, LMFT is trained in EMDR and AIT. Her website is odessawellness.com.

Roses Taylor LMFT, LPC has a website at rosestaylor.com.

Ginger Manley MSN APRH is now retired from her sex therapy practice but is Associate in Psychiatry at the Vanderbilt School of Medicine.

Betty Philips LMHC is not currently practicing.

BIBLIOGRAPHY

List of a Few Books for Children on Preventing Sexual Abuse:

Sandy Kleven, *The Right Touch: A Read-Aloud Story to Help Prevent Child Sexual Abuse* (Bellevue, Washington: Illumination Arts Publishing Company, 1998).

Lory Britain, *It's My Body (Children's Safety & Abuse Prevention)* (Seattle, WA: Parenting Press, 1984).

Cornelia Maude Spelman, *Your Body Belongs to You* (Morton Grove, IL: Albert Whitman & Company, 1997).

Amy Barth, *Annabelle's Secret: A Story about Sexual Abuse* (Ann Arbor, MI: Loving, Healing Press, 2009).

My List of the Best Books for the Healing of Adult Survivors

Ellen Bass and Laura Davis, *The Courage to Heal: A Guide for Women Survivors of Child Sexual Abuse*, 20th Anniversary Edition (New York: Collins Living, 2008).

Laura Davis, *The Courage to Heal Workbook, for Women and Men Survivors of Child Sexual Abuse* (New York: Perennial Library, 1990).

Michael Lew, *Victims No Longer: The Classic Guide for Men Recovering from Sexual Child Abuse*, 2-Sub edition (New York: Harper Paperbacks, 2004).

Other Books

Jane F. Gilgun, *What Child Sexual Abuse Means to Child Survivors* (Minneapolis, MI: Jane Gilgun Books, 2009).

BIOGRAPHY

Barbara Hughes is an artist, teacher, workshop leader and author, whose work is centered in the connections between art, spirituality and healing. She has exhibited her figurative sculptures and paintings in a variety of venues throughout the country, and her *Cathedral Nativity* is the official crèche of the Washington National Cathedral. Ms Hughes taught art and spirituality in a seminary setting for many years and now teaches in other places including Tanzania for two semesters. She leads workshops, retreats and support groups using art for women survivors of child sexual abuse from her studio, Rahamim Retreat and Clay House, and for churches and other healing centers. She does spiritual direction using art. Ms Hughes has had a touring show of the work in this book along with workshops for therapists and survivors of abuse connected to the show. Her husband is an Episcopal priest and a retired professor of theology. Ms Hughes has two sons and two grandchildren. She has a passion for eliminating childhood sexual abuse, and she believes deeply that art is a powerful force for healing in the World.

31151568R00066

Made in the USA
Charleston, SC
05 July 2014